50 Mexican Street Tacos Recipes

By: Kelly Johnson

Table of Contents

- Classic Carne Asada Tacos
- Al Pastor Tacos
- Grilled Chicken Tacos with Lime
- Shrimp Tacos with Cilantro Slaw
- Fish Tacos with Avocado Crema
- Barbacoa Beef Tacos
- Carnitas Tacos
- Tacos de Pollo (Chicken Tacos)
- Veggie Tacos with Roasted Vegetables
- Tacos de Lengua (Beef Tongue Tacos)
- Grilled Pork Tacos with Pineapple
- Tacos de Camarones (Shrimp Tacos)
- Tacos de Pescado (Fish Tacos)
- Tacos de Pollo Asado (Grilled Chicken Tacos)
- Birria Tacos
- Tacos de Chicharrón Prensado (Pressed Pork Belly Tacos)
- Tacos de Bistec (Steak Tacos)
- Spicy Tacos de Adobada
- Tacos de Tinga (Shredded Chicken in Chipotle Sauce)
- Mushroom Tacos with Cilantro-Lime Sauce
- Chorizo and Potato Tacos
- Tacos de Cochinita Pibil (Slow-Cooked Pork Tacos)
- Tacos de Frijoles (Bean Tacos)
- Sweet Potato and Black Bean Tacos
- Beef and Nopal (Cactus) Tacos
- Tacos de Sopa de Lima (Lime Soup Tacos)
- Carne Guisada Tacos (Beef Stew Tacos)
- Fish Tacos with Mango Salsa
- Grilled Veggie Tacos with Avocado
- Tacos de Pollo con Mole (Chicken with Mole Sauce)
- Bacon-Wrapped Shrimp Tacos
- Tacos de Arrachera (Skirt Steak Tacos)
- Tacos de Huevo (Egg Tacos)
- Tacos de Calabacitas (Zucchini Tacos)
- Spicy Grilled Chicken Tacos

- Tacos de Rajas Poblanas (Poblano Pepper and Cheese Tacos)
- Tacos de Pibil (Slow-Roasted Pork Tacos)
- Grilled Beef Heart Tacos
- Tacos de Pescado Baja-Style
- Guacamole and Carne Asada Tacos
- Tacos de Alambre (Grilled Meat and Veggie Tacos)
- Tacos de Pollo al Pastor (Chicken Pastor Tacos)
- Tacos de Chorizo con Papas (Chorizo and Potato Tacos)
- Tacos de Camarones a la Diabla (Spicy Shrimp Tacos)
- Tacos de Pollo con Chipotle (Chipotle Chicken Tacos)
- Lamb Barbacoa Tacos
- Tacos de Huitlacoche (Corn Mushroom Tacos)
- Tacos de Pavo (Turkey Tacos)
- Tacos de Jamón (Ham Tacos)
- Tacos de Pescado with Chipotle Mayo

Classic Carne Asada Tacos

Ingredients

- 1 lb flank steak or skirt steak
- 2 tbsp olive oil
- 2 tbsp lime juice
- 2 cloves garlic, minced
- 1 tsp cumin
- 1 tsp chili powder
- 1/2 tsp paprika
- Salt and pepper to taste
- Corn tortillas
- Toppings: chopped cilantro, diced onions, salsa, lime wedges

Instructions

1. **Marinate the Steak:**
   - In a bowl, combine olive oil, lime juice, garlic, cumin, chili powder, paprika, salt, and pepper. Place the steak in the marinade, cover, and refrigerate for at least 1 hour.
2. **Grill the Steak:**
   - Preheat the grill or a skillet over medium-high heat. Cook the steak for about 4-5 minutes per side, or until desired doneness is achieved.
3. **Slice the Steak:**
   - Let the steak rest for a few minutes before slicing thinly against the grain.
4. **Assemble the Tacos:**
   - Warm the corn tortillas, then top with the carne asada, cilantro, onions, salsa, and a squeeze of lime. Serve immediately.

Al Pastor Tacos

Ingredients

- 1 lb pork shoulder, thinly sliced
- 1/4 cup pineapple juice
- 2 tbsp chipotle in adobo sauce
- 1 tbsp white vinegar
- 1 tbsp achiote paste
- 2 cloves garlic, minced
- 1/2 tsp cumin
- 1/2 tsp paprika
- Salt and pepper to taste
- Corn tortillas
- Toppings: diced pineapple, chopped onions, cilantro, lime wedges

Instructions

1. **Marinate the Pork:**
   - In a bowl, combine pineapple juice, chipotle, vinegar, achiote paste, garlic, cumin, paprika, salt, and pepper. Add the pork slices and marinate for at least 1 hour.
2. **Cook the Pork:**
   - Heat a skillet over medium-high heat. Cook the pork for 5-7 minutes per side, or until browned and cooked through.
3. **Assemble the Tacos:**
   - Warm the tortillas and fill with the al pastor pork. Top with diced pineapple, onions, cilantro, and a squeeze of lime. Serve immediately.

Grilled Chicken Tacos with Lime

Ingredients

- 2 boneless, skinless chicken breasts
- 2 tbsp olive oil
- 2 tbsp lime juice
- 1 tsp chili powder
- 1 tsp cumin
- Salt and pepper to taste
- Corn tortillas
- Toppings: shredded lettuce, diced tomatoes, chopped cilantro, lime wedges

Instructions

1. **Marinate the Chicken:**
    - In a bowl, combine olive oil, lime juice, chili powder, cumin, salt, and pepper. Add the chicken breasts and marinate for at least 30 minutes.
2. **Grill the Chicken:**
    - Preheat the grill or a skillet over medium-high heat. Grill the chicken for 5-7 minutes per side, or until fully cooked.
3. **Slice the Chicken:**
    - Let the chicken rest for a few minutes before slicing into thin strips.
4. **Assemble the Tacos:**
    - Warm the tortillas, then top with the grilled chicken, lettuce, tomatoes, cilantro, and a squeeze of lime. Serve immediately.

Shrimp Tacos with Cilantro Slaw

Ingredients

- 1 lb shrimp, peeled and deveined
- 2 tbsp olive oil
- 1 tsp chili powder
- 1/2 tsp cumin
- Salt and pepper to taste
- Corn tortillas
- For the slaw:
    - 2 cups shredded cabbage
    - 1/4 cup chopped cilantro
    - 2 tbsp lime juice
    - 1 tbsp mayonnaise
    - Salt and pepper to taste

Instructions

1. **Prepare the Slaw:**
    - In a bowl, combine shredded cabbage, cilantro, lime juice, mayonnaise, salt, and pepper. Toss to combine.
2. **Cook the Shrimp:**
    - In a skillet, heat olive oil over medium-high heat. Season the shrimp with chili powder, cumin, salt, and pepper, and cook for 2-3 minutes per side, or until pink and cooked through.
3. **Assemble the Tacos:**
    - Warm the tortillas, then top with the shrimp and a generous portion of cilantro slaw. Serve immediately.

Fish Tacos with Avocado Crema

Ingredients

- 1 lb white fish fillets (such as tilapia or cod)
- 1 tbsp olive oil
- 1 tsp chili powder
- 1/2 tsp cumin
- Salt and pepper to taste
- Corn tortillas
- For the avocado crema:
    - 1 ripe avocado
    - 1/4 cup sour cream
    - 2 tbsp lime juice
    - 1 tbsp chopped cilantro
    - Salt to taste

Instructions

1. **Make the Avocado Crema:**
    - In a blender, combine the avocado, sour cream, lime juice, cilantro, and salt. Blend until smooth.
2. **Cook the Fish:**
    - Heat olive oil in a skillet over medium-high heat. Season the fish with chili powder, cumin, salt, and pepper, and cook for 3-4 minutes per side, or until flaky and cooked through.
3. **Assemble the Tacos:**
    - Warm the tortillas, then top with the fish and a drizzle of avocado crema. Serve immediately.

Barbacoa Beef Tacos

Ingredients

- 1 lb beef chuck roast
- 2 tbsp olive oil
- 1 onion, chopped
- 3 cloves garlic, minced
- 1 tbsp cumin
- 1 tbsp chili powder
- 1 tbsp oregano
- 1/4 cup beef broth
- 2 tbsp lime juice
- Salt and pepper to taste
- Corn tortillas
- Toppings: diced onions, chopped cilantro, lime wedges

Instructions

1. **Cook the Beef:**
    - In a pot, heat olive oil over medium-high heat. Brown the beef on all sides, then remove and set aside. Add onions and garlic to the pot and sauté until soft. Add cumin, chili powder, oregano, beef broth, and lime juice. Return the beef to the pot and cook for 3-4 hours on low heat, or until tender.
2. **Shred the Beef:**
    - Once the beef is cooked, shred it using two forks.
3. **Assemble the Tacos:**
    - Warm the tortillas, then fill with the barbacoa beef, and top with onions, cilantro, and a squeeze of lime. Serve immediately.

Carnitas Tacos

Ingredients

- 2 lb pork shoulder, cut into chunks
- 1 onion, chopped
- 2 cloves garlic, minced
- 1 tbsp cumin
- 1 tsp chili powder
- 1/2 cup orange juice
- 1/4 cup lime juice
- Salt and pepper to taste
- Corn tortillas
- Toppings: chopped cilantro, diced onions, salsa, lime wedges

Instructions

1. **Cook the Pork:**
   - In a pot or slow cooker, combine pork, onion, garlic, cumin, chili powder, orange juice, lime juice, salt, and pepper. Cook for 4-6 hours on low, or until the pork is tender.
2. **Shred the Pork:**
   - Shred the pork using two forks.
3. **Assemble the Tacos:**
   - Warm the tortillas, then top with the carnitas, cilantro, onions, and salsa. Serve immediately.

Tacos de Pollo (Chicken Tacos)

Ingredients

- 2 chicken breasts, cooked and shredded
- 2 tbsp olive oil
- 1 tsp cumin
- 1 tsp chili powder
- Salt and pepper to taste
- Corn tortillas
- Toppings: shredded lettuce, diced tomatoes, chopped cilantro, lime wedges

Instructions

1. **Season and Shred the Chicken:**
   - In a skillet, heat olive oil over medium heat. Add the shredded chicken, cumin, chili powder, salt, and pepper. Cook for 5-7 minutes, stirring to combine.
2. **Assemble the Tacos:**
   - Warm the tortillas, then top with the seasoned chicken, lettuce, tomatoes, cilantro, and a squeeze of lime. Serve immediately.

Veggie Tacos with Roasted Vegetables

Ingredients

- 1 zucchini, chopped
- 1 bell pepper, chopped
- 1 red onion, chopped
- 1 cup cherry tomatoes, halved
- 1 tbsp olive oil
- 1 tsp cumin
- 1 tsp chili powder
- Salt and pepper to taste
- Corn tortillas
- Toppings: avocado, cilantro, lime wedges, salsa

Instructions

1. **Roast the Vegetables:**
   - Preheat the oven to 400°F (200°C). Toss zucchini, bell pepper, onion, and cherry tomatoes with olive oil, cumin, chili powder, salt, and pepper. Spread them on a baking sheet and roast for 20-25 minutes, or until tender.
2. **Assemble the Tacos:**
   - Warm the tortillas and fill with the roasted vegetables. Top with avocado, cilantro, lime wedges, and salsa. Serve immediately.

Tacos de Lengua (Beef Tongue Tacos)

Ingredients

- 2 lb beef tongue
- 1 onion, quartered
- 2 cloves garlic, smashed
- 1 bay leaf
- 1 tsp cumin
- 1 tsp chili powder
- Salt and pepper to taste
- Corn tortillas
- Toppings: chopped onions, cilantro, lime wedges, salsa

Instructions

1. **Cook the Beef Tongue:**
   - Place beef tongue in a large pot with onion, garlic, bay leaf, cumin, chili powder, salt, and pepper. Cover with water and bring to a boil. Reduce to a simmer and cook for 2-3 hours, until the tongue is tender.
2. **Peel and Shred the Tongue:**
   - Let the beef tongue cool slightly. Peel off the skin and shred the meat.
3. **Assemble the Tacos:**
   - Warm the tortillas and fill with the shredded beef tongue. Top with onions, cilantro, lime wedges, and salsa. Serve immediately.

Grilled Pork Tacos with Pineapple

Ingredients

- 1 lb pork tenderloin or pork shoulder, thinly sliced
- 1 tbsp olive oil
- 1 tsp chili powder
- 1 tsp cumin
- Salt and pepper to taste
- 1/2 cup pineapple, diced
- Corn tortillas
- Toppings: cilantro, diced onions, lime wedges

Instructions

1. **Grill the Pork:**
    - Preheat the grill or a skillet over medium-high heat. Toss the sliced pork with olive oil, chili powder, cumin, salt, and pepper. Grill for 3-4 minutes per side, until cooked through.
2. **Grill the Pineapple:**
    - Grill the pineapple for 2-3 minutes until caramelized.
3. **Assemble the Tacos:**
    - Warm the tortillas, then fill with the grilled pork and pineapple. Top with cilantro, onions, and a squeeze of lime. Serve immediately.

Tacos de Camarones (Shrimp Tacos)

Ingredients

- 1 lb shrimp, peeled and deveined
- 1 tbsp olive oil
- 1 tsp cumin
- 1 tsp chili powder
- 1/2 tsp paprika
- Salt and pepper to taste
- Corn tortillas
- Toppings: avocado, cabbage slaw, cilantro, lime wedges

Instructions

1. **Cook the Shrimp:**
   - Heat olive oil in a skillet over medium-high heat. Season the shrimp with cumin, chili powder, paprika, salt, and pepper. Cook for 2-3 minutes per side, until pink and cooked through.
2. **Assemble the Tacos:**
   - Warm the tortillas, then fill with shrimp and top with avocado, cabbage slaw, cilantro, and lime wedges. Serve immediately.

Tacos de Pescado (Fish Tacos)

Ingredients

- 1 lb white fish fillets (tilapia or cod)
- 1 tbsp olive oil
- 1 tsp cumin
- 1 tsp chili powder
- Salt and pepper to taste
- Corn tortillas
- Toppings: shredded cabbage, avocado, lime wedges, cilantro

Instructions

1. **Cook the Fish:**
    - Preheat the grill or skillet over medium-high heat. Season the fish with olive oil, cumin, chili powder, salt, and pepper. Cook for 3-4 minutes per side, or until flaky.
2. **Assemble the Tacos:**
    - Warm the tortillas, then top with the fish, shredded cabbage, avocado, cilantro, and a squeeze of lime. Serve immediately.

Tacos de Pollo Asado (Grilled Chicken Tacos)

Ingredients

- 2 boneless, skinless chicken breasts
- 2 tbsp olive oil
- 2 tbsp lime juice
- 1 tsp cumin
- 1 tsp chili powder
- Salt and pepper to taste
- Corn tortillas
- Toppings: diced onions, cilantro, lime wedges

Instructions

1. **Marinate the Chicken:**
   - Combine olive oil, lime juice, cumin, chili powder, salt, and pepper in a bowl. Marinate the chicken breasts for at least 30 minutes.
2. **Grill the Chicken:**
   - Preheat the grill to medium-high heat. Grill the chicken for 5-7 minutes per side, or until fully cooked.
3. **Slice the Chicken:**
   - Let the chicken rest for a few minutes before slicing thinly.
4. **Assemble the Tacos:**
   - Warm the tortillas, then top with sliced chicken, onions, cilantro, and a squeeze of lime. Serve immediately.

Birria Tacos

Ingredients

- 2 lb beef chuck roast
- 3 dried guajillo chilies, stemmed and seeded
- 2 dried ancho chilies, stemmed and seeded
- 1 onion, quartered
- 3 cloves garlic
- 1 tbsp cumin
- 1 tbsp oregano
- 2 tsp chili powder
- 1/2 tsp cinnamon
- Salt to taste
- 4 cups beef broth
- Corn tortillas
- Toppings: diced onions, cilantro, lime wedges, salsa

Instructions

1. **Prepare the Birria:**
    - Toast the dried chilies in a skillet until fragrant, then blend them with onion, garlic, cumin, oregano, chili powder, cinnamon, salt, and beef broth until smooth.
2. **Cook the Beef:**
    - Place the beef chuck in a slow cooker and cover with the chili mixture. Cook on low for 6-8 hours, until the beef is tender and can be shredded.
3. **Shred the Beef:**
    - Shred the beef and set aside.
4. **Assemble the Tacos:**
    - Warm the tortillas, then fill with the shredded birria. Top with onions, cilantro, and a squeeze of lime. Serve with the broth on the side for dipping.

Tacos de Chicharrón Prensado (Pressed Pork Belly Tacos)

Ingredients

- 2 lb pork belly, cut into chunks
- 1 onion, chopped
- 2 cloves garlic, minced
- 1 tsp cumin
- 1 tsp oregano
- 1/2 cup orange juice
- 1/4 cup lime juice
- Corn tortillas
- Toppings: chopped onions, cilantro, salsa, lime wedges

Instructions

1. **Cook the Pork Belly:**
    - In a large pot, cook the pork belly with onion, garlic, cumin, oregano, orange juice, lime juice, salt, and pepper. Cover with water and simmer for 2-3 hours, or until the pork is tender.
2. **Press the Pork Belly:**
    - Once tender, remove the pork from the pot and shred it. Press the shredded pork with a heavy weight to compress it into a firm mass. Slice thinly.
3. **Assemble the Tacos:**
    - Warm the tortillas, then top with the pressed pork belly, onions, cilantro, and salsa. Serve immediately.

Tacos de Bistec (Steak Tacos)

Ingredients

- 1 lb flank steak or skirt steak
- 2 tbsp olive oil
- 1 tsp cumin
- 1 tsp chili powder
- Salt and pepper to taste
- Corn tortillas
- Toppings: diced onions, chopped cilantro, salsa, lime wedges

Instructions

1. **Marinate the Steak:**
    - In a bowl, combine olive oil, cumin, chili powder, salt, and pepper. Marinate the steak for at least 1 hour.
2. **Grill the Steak:**
    - Preheat the grill or skillet over medium-high heat. Grill the steak for 4-5 minutes per side, or until desired doneness.
3. **Slice the Steak:**
    - Let the steak rest before slicing thinly against the grain.
4. **Assemble the Tacos:**
    - Warm the tortillas, then top with sliced steak, onions, cilantro, salsa, and a squeeze of lime. Serve immediately.

Spicy Tacos de Adobada

Ingredients

- 1 lb pork shoulder, thinly sliced
- 3 dried guajillo chilies, stemmed and seeded
- 2 dried ancho chilies, stemmed and seeded
- 1 tbsp paprika
- 1 tbsp cumin
- 1 tbsp garlic powder
- 1/2 tsp cinnamon
- 1/4 cup vinegar
- 1/2 cup orange juice
- 1 tbsp vegetable oil
- Salt to taste
- Corn tortillas
- Toppings: pineapple slices, chopped onions, cilantro, lime wedges

Instructions

1. **Prepare the Adobada Marinade:**
    - Toast the dried chilies in a skillet until fragrant. Blend the chilies with paprika, cumin, garlic powder, cinnamon, vinegar, orange juice, salt, and a bit of water to make a smooth marinade.
2. **Marinate the Pork:**
    - Toss the pork slices in the adobada marinade and let them marinate for at least 2 hours or overnight.
3. **Cook the Pork:**
    - Heat vegetable oil in a skillet over medium-high heat. Cook the pork slices for 5-7 minutes until tender and slightly caramelized.
4. **Assemble the Tacos:**
    - Warm the tortillas, then fill with the cooked pork. Top with pineapple, onions, cilantro, and lime wedges. Serve immediately.

Tacos de Tinga (Shredded Chicken in Chipotle Sauce)

Ingredients

- 2 chicken breasts, cooked and shredded
- 2 tomatoes, chopped
- 1 onion, thinly sliced
- 2 cloves garlic, minced
- 2-3 chipotle peppers in adobo sauce
- 1 tbsp olive oil
- 1 tsp cumin
- Salt and pepper to taste
- Corn tortillas
- Toppings: chopped cilantro, avocado, lime wedges

Instructions

1. **Make the Chipotle Sauce:**
    - In a blender, combine the tomatoes, chipotle peppers, cumin, salt, and pepper. Blend until smooth.
2. **Cook the Onions and Garlic:**
    - Heat olive oil in a pan over medium heat. Add the sliced onions and garlic, cooking until softened, about 5 minutes.
3. **Add the Chicken and Sauce:**
    - Add the shredded chicken to the pan with the onions. Pour in the chipotle sauce and simmer for 10 minutes to let the flavors meld.
4. **Assemble the Tacos:**
    - Warm the tortillas, then fill with the chicken tinga. Top with cilantro, avocado, and a squeeze of lime. Serve immediately.

Mushroom Tacos with Cilantro-Lime Sauce

Ingredients

- 1 lb mushrooms, sliced (button or portobello)
- 1 tbsp olive oil
- 1 tsp cumin
- Salt and pepper to taste
- Corn tortillas
- Toppings: diced red onion, chopped cilantro, lime wedges

Cilantro-Lime Sauce:

- 1/2 cup Greek yogurt or sour cream
- 1/4 cup cilantro, chopped
- 1 tbsp lime juice
- 1 tsp garlic powder
- Salt to taste

Instructions

1. **Cook the Mushrooms:**
   - Heat olive oil in a pan over medium heat. Add the mushrooms, cumin, salt, and pepper. Cook for 7-10 minutes, until the mushrooms are tender and browned.
2. **Make the Cilantro-Lime Sauce:**
   - In a small bowl, mix together Greek yogurt, cilantro, lime juice, garlic powder, and salt. Set aside.
3. **Assemble the Tacos:**
   - Warm the tortillas, then fill with cooked mushrooms. Drizzle with the cilantro-lime sauce and top with diced onion and cilantro. Serve immediately.

Chorizo and Potato Tacos

Ingredients

- 1 lb chorizo sausage, casing removed
- 2 medium potatoes, peeled and diced
- 1 tbsp olive oil
- 1/2 onion, chopped
- 1 tsp cumin
- Salt and pepper to taste
- Corn tortillas
- Toppings: chopped cilantro, lime wedges

Instructions

1. **Cook the Potatoes:**
    - Heat olive oil in a pan over medium heat. Add diced potatoes and cook until tender and golden, about 10 minutes. Remove and set aside.
2. **Cook the Chorizo:**
    - In the same pan, cook the chorizo until browned and fully cooked, about 7-10 minutes. Add the onion and cook until softened.
3. **Combine the Potatoes and Chorizo:**
    - Add the cooked potatoes to the chorizo and stir to combine. Season with cumin, salt, and pepper.
4. **Assemble the Tacos:**
    - Warm the tortillas, then fill with the chorizo-potato mixture. Top with cilantro and a squeeze of lime. Serve immediately.

Tacos de Cochinita Pibil (Slow-Cooked Pork Tacos)

Ingredients

- 2 lb pork shoulder, cut into chunks
- 3 dried achiote peppers
- 1/4 cup orange juice
- 1/4 cup vinegar
- 1 tsp cumin
- 1 tsp oregano
- 3 cloves garlic
- 2 bay leaves
- Salt to taste
- Corn tortillas
- Toppings: pickled red onions, cilantro, lime wedges

Instructions

1. **Prepare the Achiote Marinade:**
    - Toast the achiote peppers in a skillet and blend with orange juice, vinegar, cumin, oregano, garlic, salt, and a bit of water until smooth.
2. **Slow-Cook the Pork:**
    - Place the pork chunks in a slow cooker and pour the achiote marinade over the meat. Add the bay leaves and cook on low for 6-8 hours, until the pork is tender and can be easily shredded.
3. **Shred the Pork:**
    - Once cooked, shred the pork with a fork.
4. **Assemble the Tacos:**
    - Warm the tortillas, then fill with the shredded cochinita pibil. Top with pickled onions, cilantro, and a squeeze of lime. Serve immediately.

Tacos de Frijoles (Bean Tacos)

Ingredients

- 2 cups refried beans (black or pinto beans)
- 1 tbsp olive oil
- 1/2 onion, chopped
- 1 tsp cumin
- Salt and pepper to taste
- Corn tortillas
- Toppings: shredded lettuce, diced tomatoes, cilantro, cheese (optional), salsa

Instructions

1. **Cook the Onions:**
    - Heat olive oil in a pan over medium heat. Add the chopped onions and cook until softened.
2. **Heat the Beans:**
    - Add the refried beans to the pan with the onions. Season with cumin, salt, and pepper. Heat for 5-7 minutes, stirring occasionally.
3. **Assemble the Tacos:**
    - Warm the tortillas, then fill with the bean mixture. Top with lettuce, tomatoes, cilantro, cheese, and salsa. Serve immediately.

Sweet Potato and Black Bean Tacos

Ingredients

- 2 medium sweet potatoes, peeled and diced
- 1 tbsp olive oil
- 1 tsp cumin
- 1 tsp chili powder
- Salt and pepper to taste
- 1 can black beans, drained and rinsed
- Corn tortillas
- Toppings: avocado, cilantro, lime wedges, salsa

Instructions

1. **Roast the Sweet Potatoes:**
    - Preheat the oven to 400°F (200°C). Toss the diced sweet potatoes with olive oil, cumin, chili powder, salt, and pepper. Roast for 20-25 minutes until tender.
2. **Heat the Beans:**
    - While the sweet potatoes roast, heat the black beans in a small pot over low heat until warmed.
3. **Assemble the Tacos:**
    - Warm the tortillas, then fill with roasted sweet potatoes and black beans. Top with avocado, cilantro, lime wedges, and salsa. Serve immediately.

Beef and Nopal (Cactus) Tacos

Ingredients

- 1 lb flank steak or skirt steak
- 2 cactus pads (nopales), sliced into strips
- 1 tbsp olive oil
- 1 tsp cumin
- 1 tsp chili powder
- Salt and pepper to taste
- Corn tortillas
- Toppings: chopped onions, cilantro, lime wedges

Instructions

1. **Cook the Beef:**
    - Preheat the grill or skillet over medium-high heat. Season the beef with cumin, chili powder, salt, and pepper. Grill for 4-5 minutes per side, until desired doneness.
2. **Cook the Nopales:**
    - In a separate skillet, heat olive oil and cook the sliced cactus strips for 5-7 minutes, until tender.
3. **Assemble the Tacos:**
    - Warm the tortillas, then fill with sliced beef and cactus. Top with onions, cilantro, and a squeeze of lime. Serve immediately.

Tacos de Sopa de Lima (Lime Soup Tacos)

Ingredients

- 2 chicken breasts, cooked and shredded
- 6 cups chicken broth
- 2 limes, juiced and zested
- 1 onion, chopped
- 2 cloves garlic, minced
- 2 tomatoes, chopped
- 1 tsp cumin
- 1 tsp oregano
- 2 tbsp vegetable oil
- Corn tortillas
- Toppings: crispy tortilla strips, avocado, cilantro, lime wedges

Instructions

1. **Prepare the Soup Base:**
    - In a large pot, heat vegetable oil over medium heat. Add chopped onion and garlic, cooking until softened. Add tomatoes, cumin, oregano, and cook for 5 minutes.
2. **Add Chicken and Broth:**
    - Add chicken broth, shredded chicken, lime juice, and lime zest. Bring to a boil, then reduce heat and simmer for 15-20 minutes.
3. **Assemble the Tacos:**
    - Warm the tortillas, then ladle some of the soup mixture (with chicken and broth) onto the tortillas. Top with crispy tortilla strips, avocado, cilantro, and lime wedges. Serve immediately.

Carne Guisada Tacos (Beef Stew Tacos)

Ingredients

- 2 lbs beef stew meat, cut into cubes
- 2 tbsp vegetable oil
- 1 onion, chopped
- 3 cloves garlic, minced
- 2 tomatoes, chopped
- 1 cup beef broth
- 1 tsp cumin
- 1 tsp chili powder
- Salt and pepper to taste
- Corn tortillas
- Toppings: chopped cilantro, diced onions, lime wedges

Instructions

1. **Brown the Beef:**
    - Heat oil in a large pot over medium-high heat. Brown the beef cubes on all sides. Remove the beef and set aside.
2. **Cook the Onions and Garlic:**
    - In the same pot, cook the onions and garlic until softened. Add the tomatoes, cumin, chili powder, salt, and pepper. Cook for 5 minutes.
3. **Simmer the Stew:**
    - Return the beef to the pot, add beef broth, and bring to a boil. Reduce heat and simmer for 1-1.5 hours, or until the beef is tender.
4. **Assemble the Tacos:**
    - Warm the tortillas, then fill with the beef stew. Top with cilantro, diced onions, and a squeeze of lime. Serve immediately.

Fish Tacos with Mango Salsa

Ingredients

- 1 lb white fish fillets (such as cod or tilapia)
- 1 tbsp olive oil
- 1 tsp cumin
- 1 tsp paprika
- Salt and pepper to taste
- Corn tortillas
- **Mango Salsa:**
    - 1 mango, diced
    - 1/4 red onion, diced
    - 1 jalapeño, minced
    - 1/4 cup cilantro, chopped
    - 1 tbsp lime juice
    - Salt to taste

Instructions

1. **Prepare the Mango Salsa:**
    - In a bowl, combine the mango, red onion, jalapeño, cilantro, lime juice, and salt. Mix well and set aside.
2. **Cook the Fish:**
    - Preheat a skillet over medium heat and drizzle with olive oil. Season the fish fillets with cumin, paprika, salt, and pepper. Cook the fish for 2-3 minutes per side until golden and cooked through. Flake the fish with a fork.
3. **Assemble the Tacos:**
    - Warm the tortillas, then fill with the flaked fish. Top with mango salsa and a squeeze of lime. Serve immediately.

Grilled Veggie Tacos with Avocado

Ingredients

- 2 zucchini, sliced
- 1 bell pepper, sliced
- 1 red onion, sliced
- 1 tbsp olive oil
- 1 tsp chili powder
- Salt and pepper to taste
- 1 avocado, sliced
- Corn tortillas
- Toppings: cilantro, lime wedges

Instructions

1. **Grill the Vegetables:**
    - Preheat the grill or grill pan over medium heat. Toss the zucchini, bell pepper, and onion with olive oil, chili powder, salt, and pepper. Grill for 5-7 minutes until tender and slightly charred.
2. **Assemble the Tacos:**
    - Warm the tortillas, then fill with the grilled vegetables. Top with avocado slices, cilantro, and a squeeze of lime. Serve immediately.

Tacos de Pollo con Mole (Chicken with Mole Sauce)

Ingredients

- 2 chicken breasts, cooked and shredded
- 1 cup mole sauce (store-bought or homemade)
- Corn tortillas
- Toppings: chopped onions, cilantro, sesame seeds

Instructions

1. **Warm the Mole Sauce:**
   - In a saucepan, heat the mole sauce over low heat until warmed through.
2. **Combine the Chicken and Mole:**
   - Add the shredded chicken to the mole sauce and stir to coat. Simmer for 5-10 minutes.
3. **Assemble the Tacos:**
   - Warm the tortillas, then fill with the chicken and mole sauce. Top with chopped onions, cilantro, and sesame seeds. Serve immediately.

Bacon-Wrapped Shrimp Tacos

Ingredients

- 1 lb shrimp, peeled and deveined
- 8 strips of bacon
- 1 tsp chili powder
- 1 tsp paprika
- Salt and pepper to taste
- Corn tortillas
- Toppings: avocado, cilantro, lime wedges

Instructions

1. **Wrap the Shrimp:**
    - Wrap each shrimp with a strip of bacon and secure with a toothpick. Season with chili powder, paprika, salt, and pepper.
2. **Cook the Shrimp:**
    - Heat a skillet over medium heat. Cook the bacon-wrapped shrimp for 2-3 minutes per side until the bacon is crispy and the shrimp are cooked through.
3. **Assemble the Tacos:**
    - Warm the tortillas, then fill with the bacon-wrapped shrimp. Top with avocado, cilantro, and a squeeze of lime. Serve immediately.

Tacos de Arrachera (Skirt Steak Tacos)

Ingredients

- 1 lb skirt steak
- 2 tbsp olive oil
- 2 cloves garlic, minced
- 1 tsp cumin
- 1 tsp chili powder
- Salt and pepper to taste
- Corn tortillas
- Toppings: chopped onions, cilantro, lime wedges

Instructions

1. **Marinate the Skirt Steak:**
   - Rub the skirt steak with olive oil, garlic, cumin, chili powder, salt, and pepper. Let it marinate for at least 30 minutes.
2. **Grill the Steak:**
   - Preheat the grill or skillet over high heat. Grill the skirt steak for 3-4 minutes per side for medium-rare, or to your desired doneness. Let it rest for 5 minutes before slicing thinly.
3. **Assemble the Tacos:**
   - Warm the tortillas, then fill with the sliced skirt steak. Top with chopped onions, cilantro, and a squeeze of lime. Serve immediately.

Tacos de Huevo (Egg Tacos)

Ingredients

- 4 eggs, scrambled
- 1 tbsp olive oil
- Salt and pepper to taste
- Corn tortillas
- Toppings: salsa, avocado, cilantro

Instructions

1. **Scramble the Eggs:**
    - Heat olive oil in a skillet over medium heat. Scramble the eggs with salt and pepper until cooked through.
2. **Assemble the Tacos:**
    - Warm the tortillas, then fill with scrambled eggs. Top with salsa, avocado, and cilantro. Serve immediately.

Tacos de Calabacitas (Zucchini Tacos)

Ingredients

- 2 zucchinis, sliced
- 1 onion, sliced
- 1 tbsp olive oil
- 1 tsp cumin
- 1 tsp chili powder
- Salt and pepper to taste
- Corn tortillas
- Toppings: queso fresco, cilantro, lime wedges

Instructions

1. **Cook the Zucchini:**
   - Heat olive oil in a skillet over medium heat. Add the zucchini and onion slices, cooking until tender, about 5-7 minutes. Season with cumin, chili powder, salt, and pepper.
2. **Assemble the Tacos:**
   - Warm the tortillas, then fill with the sautéed zucchini and onion mixture. Top with crumbled queso fresco, cilantro, and a squeeze of lime. Serve immediately.

Spicy Grilled Chicken Tacos

Ingredients

- 2 chicken breasts
- 1 tbsp olive oil
- 2 cloves garlic, minced
- 1 tbsp chili powder
- 1 tsp paprika
- 1 tsp cumin
- 1 tsp cayenne pepper
- Salt and pepper to taste
- Corn tortillas
- Toppings: salsa, avocado, cilantro, lime wedges

Instructions

1. **Marinate the Chicken:**
    - In a bowl, combine olive oil, garlic, chili powder, paprika, cumin, cayenne pepper, salt, and pepper. Coat the chicken breasts in the marinade and refrigerate for at least 30 minutes.
2. **Grill the Chicken:**
    - Preheat the grill or grill pan to medium-high heat. Grill the chicken for 6-8 minutes per side, or until fully cooked. Let rest for 5 minutes before slicing.
3. **Assemble the Tacos:**
    - Warm the tortillas, then fill with sliced grilled chicken. Top with salsa, avocado, cilantro, and a squeeze of lime. Serve immediately.

Tacos de Rajas Poblanas (Poblano Pepper and Cheese Tacos)

Ingredients

- 2 poblano peppers, roasted and sliced
- 1 onion, sliced
- 1 tbsp olive oil
- 1 tsp cumin
- 1/2 cup shredded cheese (Oaxaca or Monterey Jack)
- Corn tortillas
- Toppings: sour cream, cilantro, lime wedges

Instructions

1. **Prepare the Poblano Peppers:**
   - Roast the poblano peppers until the skin is charred, then peel and slice. Set aside.
2. **Sauté the Onions:**
   - Heat olive oil in a skillet over medium heat. Sauté the sliced onion until softened, about 5 minutes.
3. **Combine the Ingredients:**
   - Add the roasted poblano peppers to the skillet with the onions and sprinkle with cumin. Cook for another 2 minutes.
4. **Assemble the Tacos:**
   - Warm the tortillas, then fill with the poblano pepper and onion mixture. Top with shredded cheese, sour cream, cilantro, and a squeeze of lime. Serve immediately.

Tacos de Pibil (Slow-Roasted Pork Tacos)

Ingredients

- 2 lbs pork shoulder, cut into chunks
- 1/4 cup achiote paste
- 1/4 cup orange juice
- 2 cloves garlic, minced
- 1 tbsp cumin
- 1 tsp oregano
- Salt and pepper to taste
- Banana leaves or foil for wrapping
- Corn tortillas
- Toppings: pickled red onions, cilantro, lime wedges

Instructions

1. **Prepare the Pork:**
    - In a bowl, combine achiote paste, orange juice, garlic, cumin, oregano, salt, and pepper. Coat the pork chunks with the marinade and refrigerate for at least 2 hours.
2. **Slow-Cook the Pork:**
    - Preheat the oven to 300°F (150°C). Wrap the marinated pork in banana leaves or foil and roast for 3-4 hours, until tender and easily shredable.
3. **Assemble the Tacos:**
    - Shred the pork and warm the tortillas. Fill the tortillas with the pulled pork and top with pickled red onions, cilantro, and a squeeze of lime. Serve immediately.

Grilled Beef Heart Tacos

Ingredients

- 1 beef heart, cleaned and trimmed
- 2 tbsp olive oil
- 2 cloves garlic, minced
- 1 tbsp chili powder
- 1 tsp cumin
- 1 tsp paprika
- Salt and pepper to taste
- Corn tortillas
- Toppings: salsa, avocado, cilantro, lime wedges

Instructions

1. **Prepare the Beef Heart:**
    - Slice the beef heart into thin strips. Rub with olive oil, garlic, chili powder, cumin, paprika, salt, and pepper.
2. **Grill the Beef Heart:**
    - Preheat the grill to medium-high heat. Grill the beef heart strips for 2-3 minutes per side, until cooked through.
3. **Assemble the Tacos:**
    - Warm the tortillas, then fill with the grilled beef heart. Top with salsa, avocado, cilantro, and a squeeze of lime. Serve immediately.

Tacos de Pescado Baja-Style (Baja Fish Tacos)

Ingredients

- 1 lb white fish fillets (such as cod or tilapia)
- 1/2 cup flour
- 1 tsp chili powder
- 1 tsp paprika
- 1 tsp cumin
- Salt and pepper to taste
- 1/2 cup beer (optional)
- Corn tortillas
- Toppings: cabbage slaw, crema, cilantro, lime wedges

Instructions

1. **Prepare the Fish:**
   - Cut the fish fillets into bite-sized pieces. In a bowl, mix flour, chili powder, paprika, cumin, salt, and pepper. Dip the fish pieces into the flour mixture, then into the beer.
2. **Fry the Fish:**
   - Heat oil in a skillet over medium-high heat. Fry the battered fish pieces for 3-4 minutes per side, until golden and crispy. Remove from the skillet and drain on paper towels.
3. **Assemble the Tacos:**
   - Warm the tortillas, then fill with the fried fish. Top with cabbage slaw, crema, cilantro, and a squeeze of lime. Serve immediately.

Guacamole and Carne Asada Tacos

Ingredients

- 1 lb flank steak or skirt steak
- 2 tbsp olive oil
- 2 cloves garlic, minced
- 1 tsp cumin
- Salt and pepper to taste
- Corn tortillas
- **Guacamole:**
    - 2 ripe avocados, mashed
    - 1/4 red onion, diced
    - 1 jalapeño, minced
    - 1 tbsp lime juice
    - Salt to taste
- Toppings: cilantro, lime wedges

Instructions

1. **Marinate the Steak:**
    - Rub the steak with olive oil, garlic, cumin, salt, and pepper. Let it marinate for at least 30 minutes.
2. **Grill the Steak:**
    - Preheat the grill to medium-high heat. Grill the steak for 4-5 minutes per side, or until your desired doneness. Let it rest before slicing thinly against the grain.
3. **Prepare the Guacamole:**
    - In a bowl, combine mashed avocados, red onion, jalapeño, lime juice, and salt.
4. **Assemble the Tacos:**
    - Warm the tortillas, then fill with the sliced carne asada. Top with guacamole, cilantro, and a squeeze of lime. Serve immediately.

Tacos de Alambre (Grilled Meat and Veggie Tacos)

Ingredients

- 1 lb beef, chicken, or pork (your choice), cut into small pieces
- 1 bell pepper, sliced
- 1 onion, sliced
- 2 tbsp olive oil
- 1 tsp chili powder
- 1 tsp cumin
- Salt and pepper to taste
- Corn tortillas
- Toppings: shredded cheese, salsa, cilantro, lime wedges

Instructions

1. **Cook the Meat and Vegetables:**
    - Heat olive oil in a skillet over medium-high heat. Add the meat and cook until browned and cooked through. Add the bell pepper and onion slices and cook for an additional 5 minutes. Season with chili powder, cumin, salt, and pepper.
2. **Assemble the Tacos:**
    - Warm the tortillas, then fill with the cooked meat and vegetable mixture. Top with shredded cheese, salsa, cilantro, and a squeeze of lime. Serve immediately.

Tacos de Pollo al Pastor (Chicken Pastor Tacos)

Ingredients

- 2 chicken breasts, sliced thinly
- 1/4 cup achiote paste
- 1/4 cup pineapple juice
- 2 tbsp vinegar
- 2 cloves garlic, minced
- 1 tbsp chili powder
- 1 tsp cumin
- 1/2 tsp oregano
- Salt and pepper to taste
- Corn tortillas
- Toppings: pineapple chunks, cilantro, lime wedges, sliced onions

Instructions

1. **Marinate the Chicken:**
   - In a bowl, combine achiote paste, pineapple juice, vinegar, garlic, chili powder, cumin, oregano, salt, and pepper. Marinate the chicken for at least 30 minutes.
2. **Cook the Chicken:**
   - Heat a grill or skillet over medium heat. Cook the chicken slices for 5-7 minutes on each side, until fully cooked.
3. **Assemble the Tacos:**
   - Warm the tortillas and fill with the cooked chicken. Top with pineapple chunks, cilantro, sliced onions, and a squeeze of lime. Serve immediately.

Tacos de Chorizo con Papas (Chorizo and Potato Tacos)

Ingredients

- 1 lb chorizo sausage
- 2 medium potatoes, peeled and diced
- 1/2 onion, diced
- 1 tbsp olive oil
- Salt and pepper to taste
- Corn tortillas
- Toppings: cilantro, lime wedges, salsa

Instructions

1. **Cook the Potatoes:**
    - Heat olive oil in a skillet over medium heat. Add the diced potatoes and cook until golden and tender, about 10-12 minutes. Remove and set aside.
2. **Cook the Chorizo:**
    - In the same skillet, cook the chorizo until fully browned, breaking it apart as it cooks. Add the cooked potatoes and diced onion. Season with salt and pepper. Stir to combine and cook for an additional 5 minutes.
3. **Assemble the Tacos:**
    - Warm the tortillas and fill with the chorizo and potato mixture. Top with cilantro, lime wedges, and salsa. Serve immediately.

Tacos de Camarones a la Diabla (Spicy Shrimp Tacos)

Ingredients

- 1 lb shrimp, peeled and deveined
- 2 tbsp olive oil
- 2 cloves garlic, minced
- 2 tbsp chipotle peppers in adobo sauce, chopped
- 1 tsp smoked paprika
- 1/2 tsp cayenne pepper
- Salt and pepper to taste
- Corn tortillas
- Toppings: cabbage slaw, avocado, cilantro, lime wedges

Instructions

1. **Prepare the Shrimp:**
   - Heat olive oil in a skillet over medium heat. Add the garlic and cook for 1 minute. Stir in the chipotle peppers, paprika, cayenne pepper, salt, and pepper. Cook for another 2 minutes.
2. **Cook the Shrimp:**
   - Add the shrimp to the skillet and cook for 3-4 minutes, until pink and cooked through.
3. **Assemble the Tacos:**
   - Warm the tortillas and fill with the spicy shrimp. Top with cabbage slaw, avocado, cilantro, and a squeeze of lime. Serve immediately.

Tacos de Pollo con Chipotle (Chipotle Chicken Tacos)

Ingredients

- 2 chicken breasts, cut into strips
- 1 chipotle pepper in adobo sauce, minced
- 1 tbsp adobo sauce
- 1 tbsp olive oil
- 1 tsp cumin
- 1 tsp garlic powder
- Salt and pepper to taste
- Corn tortillas
- Toppings: sour cream, avocado, cilantro, lime wedges

Instructions

1. **Marinate the Chicken:**
   - In a bowl, mix the chipotle pepper, adobo sauce, olive oil, cumin, garlic powder, salt, and pepper. Add the chicken strips and marinate for at least 30 minutes.
2. **Cook the Chicken:**
   - Heat a skillet over medium-high heat. Cook the chicken strips for 5-7 minutes, or until cooked through.
3. **Assemble the Tacos:**
   - Warm the tortillas and fill with the chipotle chicken. Top with sour cream, avocado, cilantro, and a squeeze of lime. Serve immediately.

Lamb Barbacoa Tacos

Ingredients

- 2 lbs lamb shoulder, cut into chunks
- 2 tbsp olive oil
- 1 onion, sliced
- 2 cloves garlic, minced
- 1 tbsp cumin
- 1 tbsp oregano
- 1 tbsp chili powder
- 1/4 cup apple cider vinegar
- 1 cup beef broth
- Salt and pepper to taste
- Corn tortillas
- Toppings: cilantro, lime wedges, diced onions

Instructions

1. **Prepare the Lamb:**
    - Heat olive oil in a large pot over medium-high heat. Brown the lamb chunks on all sides, then remove and set aside.
2. **Cook the Aromatics:**
    - In the same pot, sauté the onion and garlic until softened. Add the cumin, oregano, chili powder, salt, and pepper. Stir to combine.
3. **Simmer the Lamb:**
    - Return the lamb to the pot, add apple cider vinegar, beef broth, and bring to a simmer. Cover and cook for 2-3 hours, until the lamb is tender and easily shreds.
4. **Assemble the Tacos:**
    - Shred the lamb and warm the tortillas. Fill the tortillas with the shredded lamb and top with cilantro, diced onions, and a squeeze of lime. Serve immediately.

Tacos de Huitlacoche (Corn Mushroom Tacos)

Ingredients

- 1 can huitlacoche (corn mushroom) or fresh huitlacoche, if available
- 1 tbsp olive oil
- 1/2 onion, diced
- 2 cloves garlic, minced
- 1 tsp cumin
- Salt and pepper to taste
- Corn tortillas
- Toppings: queso fresco, cilantro, lime wedges

Instructions

1. **Prepare the Huitlacoche:**
    - Heat olive oil in a skillet over medium heat. Sauté the onion and garlic until softened. Add the huitlacoche and cook for 5-7 minutes, seasoning with cumin, salt, and pepper.
2. **Assemble the Tacos:**
    - Warm the tortillas and fill with the huitlacoche mixture. Top with crumbled queso fresco, cilantro, and a squeeze of lime. Serve immediately.

Tacos de Pavo (Turkey Tacos)

Ingredients

- 1 lb ground turkey
- 1 tbsp olive oil
- 1 tsp cumin
- 1 tsp chili powder
- 1 tsp garlic powder
- Salt and pepper to taste
- Corn tortillas
- Toppings: lettuce, tomato, cheese, salsa, cilantro

Instructions

1. **Cook the Turkey:**
    - Heat olive oil in a skillet over medium-high heat. Add the ground turkey and cook until browned. Stir in the cumin, chili powder, garlic powder, salt, and pepper.
2. **Assemble the Tacos:**
    - Warm the tortillas and fill with the cooked turkey. Top with lettuce, tomato, cheese, salsa, and cilantro. Serve immediately.

Tacos de Jamón (Ham Tacos)

Ingredients

- 1 lb ham, sliced thinly
- 1 tbsp olive oil
- 1/2 onion, sliced
- 1 tsp mustard (optional)
- Salt and pepper to taste
- Corn tortillas
- Toppings: avocado, cilantro, lime wedges

Instructions

1. **Prepare the Ham:**
   - Heat olive oil in a skillet over medium heat. Add the sliced ham and cook for 3-5 minutes until heated through. Optionally, add a bit of mustard for flavor.
2. **Assemble the Tacos:**
   - Warm the tortillas and fill with the cooked ham. Top with avocado, cilantro, and a squeeze of lime. Serve immediately.

Tacos de Pescado with Chipotle Mayo

Ingredients

- 1 lb white fish fillets (such as cod or tilapia)
- 1/2 cup flour
- 1 tsp paprika
- 1 tsp cumin
- Salt and pepper to taste
- 1/2 cup mayonnaise
- 2 tbsp chipotle peppers in adobo sauce, minced
- Corn tortillas
- Toppings: cabbage slaw, avocado, cilantro, lime wedges

Instructions

1. **Prepare the Fish:**
   - Coat the fish fillets in a mixture of flour, paprika, cumin, salt, and pepper.
2. **Fry the Fish:**
   - Heat oil in a skillet over medium-high heat. Fry the coated fish fillets for 3-4 minutes per side, until golden and crispy.
3. **Make the Chipotle Mayo:**
   - In a bowl, combine mayonnaise and chipotle peppers in adobo sauce.
4. **Assemble the Tacos:**
   - Warm the tortillas and fill with the fried fish. Top with cabbage slaw, avocado, cilantro, and a drizzle of chipotle mayo. Serve immediately.

www.ingramcontent.com/pod-product-compliance
Lightning Source LLC
LaVergne TN
LVHW081342060526
838201LV00055B/2799